Writing for Recovery

Daily Exercises for Reflection

Sam Louie, MA, LMHC

Writing for Recovery: Daily Exercises for Reflection
Copyright 2015 Sam Louie

ISBN-13: 9781530311934
ISBN-10: 1530311934

Cover and Interior Design by Penoaks Publishing, http://penoaks.com

As a therapist in private practice specializing in sex addiction, I've noticed clients who read and write not only learn more about themselves but tend to stay sober longer.

You can't just stop an activity but must replace it with something healthy and positive. Consequently, I've compiled this book of daily journaling questions for you to answer and reflect upon. If you're intimidated by writing, don't be. I've made this as simple as possible by providing you with blank pages to write your thoughts as they occur. You can answer the question by writing as much or as little as possible. Occasionally there will be non-writing exercises to break up the monotony of writing. The goal is to learn to embrace solitude and the inner thoughts that arise since addicts have learned to suppress, hide, or deny their thoughts and feelings.

Remember that writing works a different part of the brain than simply speaking. It is for this reason that I ask clients to write, as you will garner a much deeper emotional reservoir that you thought possible. In addition, after time you will hopefully see connections from your answers to your addiction.

May your journey of recovery be blessed by a newfound appreciation of your growth, perseverance, and resiliency.

Sincerely,
Sam Louie, MA, LMHC
www.samlouiemft.com
sam@samlouiemft.com
(206) 778-2686

January 1

What specific behaviors make-up your compulsive/addictive acting-out patterns?

January 2

How have you been pre-occupied with sex (or other addiction)? Please start with early childhood experiences, fantasies, memories.

January 3

How have you lied about your sexual activities to your partner?

January 4

What are some rationales you gave to justify your sexual behaviors? (i.e. entitlement, blaming spouse, reward, stress-reliever)

January 5

How was love expressed to you as a child?

January 6

Were your parents physically affectionate
(loves, kisses, hugs, etc.)? If not, why do you
think this was so?

3

January 7
How did culture (ethnic, popular culture, media, etc.) impact your view of sexual behaviors?

January 8
Whom did you admire as sexual role-models (i.e. Hollywood, fairy tales, etc.)?

January 9

Were there affairs or sexual secrets in your
family of origin? What about secrets in
general? Was the family mantra, "we don't air
our dirty laundry?"

January 10

In what ways did you experience neglect
(emotional or physical), rejection, or losses
growing up?

January 11

In what ways did you experience physical or sexual abuse? If this doesn't apply, how was disciplined communicated to you? Was the punishment fair compared to the "crime"?

January 12

Describe your early feelings toward girls/women?

January 13

Describe some of your early experiences of sexual arousal and feelings surrounding them?

January 14

Describe what you can recall of your first masturbation experience. (i.e. fantasy content, feelings, the context)

January 15

What did your parents teach you about sex?

January 16

If from a religious or ethnic upbringing, what
was taught about sex?

January 17
How did you view your sense of self-worth,
adequacy, and competence growing up?

January 18
How unpredictable was parental discipline
growing up? (i.e. yelling, spanking, hitting, etc.)
Or was it non-existent or too lax?

January 19

When you experience strong or intense feelings in childhood (i.e. fear, anger, sadness, frustration, etc.) how did you handle them?

January 20

Were you ever teased or harassed about being different?

January 21

How comfortable were you with girls your age growing up?

January 22

Was it easy to ask girls out/have girlfriends?

January 23

Did you like your body? What parts (if any) did you find shameful? How much was related to your culture, ethnicity?

January 24

How was body image communicated within your family or culture (i.e. cultural scripts)?

January 25

Dating & Marriage: what are the rules regarding dating and marriage? Were any relatives in an arranged marriage? How did this impact them and you? What cultural expectations are there for you when it comes to relationships (i.e. marrying within your ethnicity, social class, etc.)?

January 26

*How do you want this year to be different
from last year in your recovery?*

January 27

*What changes will you make to reach that
goal?*

January 28
Why did you decide to get help?

January 29
Do you feel pressured to get better? Why or why not?

January 30

*How have you been able to live a secret life
(i.e. keep your behaviors hidden from others)?*

January 31

*Do you believe you can recovery from your
addiction? Why or why not?*

February 1

How bleak does your life feel right now?

February 2

What have you told yourself in the past to rationalize your actions?

February 3

How much is collectivism a part of your family/culture (i.e. the need to put the group ahead of the individual)?

February 4

What message did your parents tell you either explicitly or implicitly when it came to sharing of emotions? Why do you think this was so? How did you handle it in childhood?

February 5

What unique pressures do you face coming from your background that may be different from others?

February 6

"Saving face" is a concept to not bring shame upon yourself or family so how has this concept impacted you and your addiction?

February 7

Shame is defined as feeling that you as a person are flawed, defective or a mistake (e.g. "I'm a mistake" vs. "I made a mistake"), how much does this resonate with you? What are some of your earliest memories of feeling this way?

February 8

What is it like sharing these aspects of your shame now with others?

February 9

Since shame and honor are intricately tied together in many families and cultures, how have you tried to present an "honorable" image to others?

February 10

Do you feel you are "dishonoring" your parents or culture when revealing aspects of your life that are shameful?

February 11

What areas in your life do you find shameful to share (e.g. academics, education, career, relationships, body image, sexual self, etc)? Why is this so?

February 12

Most clients in therapy repeatedly received messages that denied their feelings and invalidated their experience. Some examples of these messages include:

- You shouldn't feel that way.
- Why would a silly thing like that make you mad?
- We don't talk about those things.
- You can't possibly be hungry now.
- How can you be tired? You've hardly done anything.
- You shouldn't be upset at your mother. She loves you very much.
- You don't really want to talk about that.
- What's the matter with you? How could you feel that way!

Which of the above statements were true in your family? What others not listed come to mind? How do you feel about this invalidation of your feelings?

24

February 13
How did your parents express love?

February 14
Did they tell you they loved you?

February 15

Did you receive hugs growing up?

February 16

*Did you receive praise just for being you? (i.e.
Did praise only come when you did something
well?)*

February 17

Where you were born, did you move around much, and what your family do for a living? How do you think these conditions impacted you?

February 18

How would you describe your relationship with your parents as a young child (thinking as far back as you can remember up to pre-adolescent years)?

February 19

What five adjectives or words best reflect your relationship with your mother starting from as far back as you can remember in early childhood. Now go back and write a reason for each adjective you chose and what particular incident or memory influenced that choice.☐

February 20

What five adjectives or words best reflect
your relationship with your father starting
from as far back as you can remember in
early childhood. Now go back and write a
reason for each adjective you chose and what
particular incident or memory influenced that
choice.☐

February 21

Which parent did you feel the closest, and
why? Why isn't there this feeling with the
other parent?

February 22

When you were upset emotionally when you
were little, what would you do? Can you think
of a specific time that happened?

February 23

Can you remember what would happen when you were hurt physically? Again, do any specific incidents (or do any other incidents) come to mind?

February 24

Were you ever ill when you were little? Do you remember what would happen?

February 25

Do you remember being held by either of your parents at any of these times--when you were upset, or hurt, or ill? If you have children, do you hold them when they're upset, hurt, or ill? Why or why not?

February 26

What is the first time you remember being separated from your parents? How did you respond?

February 27

Did you ever feel rejected by your parents as a young child? How old were you and what were the circumstances?

February 28

Why do you think your parent did those things--do you think he/she realized he/she was rejecting you?

March 1

Were you ever frightened or worried as a
child? What were the circumstances? Did you
share these feelings with anyone? Why or why
not?

March 2

Were your parents ever threatening with you
in any way - maybe for discipline, or even
jokingly? How do you feel about it when
reflecting back on this?

March 3

Were you ever abused physically or sexually?
Describe the circumstances and feelings both
then and now.

March 4

How do you think your overall experiences
with your parents have affected your adult
personality?

March 5

Are there any aspects to your early experiences that you feel were a setback in your development?

March 6

Did a parent or other adult in the household swear at you, insult you, put you down, humiliate or act in a way that made you afraid that you might be physically hurt? If so, how did it make you feel?

March 7

Did a parent or other adult in the household push, grab, slap, or throw something at you or ☐ever hit you so hard that you had marks or were injured? If so, how did it make you feel?

March 8

How did your family love you or make you feel you were important or special?

March 9

The first thing I ever remember was....

March 10

The things that made me mad as a child were...

March 11

I hated it when my mother...

March 12

I loved it when my mother...

March 13

I hated it when my father...

March 14

I loved it when my father...

March 15
I wish I learned how to...

March 16
My favorite food as a child...

41

March 17

When I was a child I especially hated...

March 18

When I was a child, more than anything I loved...

March 19

My best friend in childhood made me mad
when...

March 20

It really bothered me in childhood when...

March 21

As a child I was scared of...

March 22

The thing I loved about growing up in my (neighborhood, city, country, etc.)...

March 23

The thing I hated about growing up in my
(neighborhood, city, country, etc.)...

March 24

At recess, I loved...

March 25

At recess, I hated...

March 26

The saddest thing to happen to me was...

March 27

The best thing to happen to me was...

March 28

As a child I hated it when my parents made me....

March 29

As a child I loved it when my parents made me...

March 30

The fun things I did each summer were...

March 31

The most important adult in my life other than my family is....(please explain why)

April 1

The thing I worried about most as a child was...

49

April 2

The most embarrassing thing to happen to me as a child was....

April 3

Sometimes I felt different because...

April 4

What I'd like from my childhood to do over again is....

April 5

My favorite books were....

April 6

As a child, my favorite tv shows/movies were...

April 7

The feelings that came easily to me as a child...

April 8

The feelings that come easily to me as an adult...

April 9

The feelings which are hard for me to access as an adult...

April 10
Why is it hard to access certain feelings?

April 11
What emotional triggers can impact me the most to act-out sexually?

April 12

What visual triggers can impact me to act-out?

April 13

What environmental triggers can impact me to act-out?

April 14
What relational triggers can impact me to act-out?

April 15
How has denial been used to hide the addiction?

April 16

How have I made excuses to give myself reason to act-out?

April 17

How have I justified my past sexual behaviors?

April 18

Who have I blamed to allow me to continue my addiction?

April 19

How have I either blatantly lied about my addiction or used a lie of omission?

April 20

How have I used "diversion" techniques to steer a conversation away from my issue and onto something else as a means of taking the attention away from me?

April 21

How have I minimized my compulsive sexual behaviors?

April 22

How have I used anger to manipulate, control, and divert attention toward others?

April 23

How have I "kept score" (i.e. keeping track of mistakes others) as a way to avoid taking responsibility for my actions and thus blame others when I'm criticized?

April 24

The addict will often want to present himself/herself as a victim in order to manipulate and control others. This is a form of passive- aggressive behavior and it is often exerted toward people who care about the addict. How have you taken the "victim stance" in your past?

April 25

All-or-nothing thinking — seeing things as all good or all bad and allowing for no middle ground. How have I used "all-or-nothing thinking" (i.e. black/white thinking) to impact me?

April 26

Over-generalizing — reaching a general
conclusion based on a single incident or piece
of evidence; creating assumptions about
events or outcomes solely because of past
experience. How have I over-generalized when
it comes to my addiction?

April 27

Catastrophizing — exaggerating the impact of events and convincing yourself that if something goes wrong, it will be intolerable and you will relapse. (e.g. "Without sex, I won't be able to handle my nervousness and stress.") How have I catastrophized my addiction?

April 28

Taking it Personally — blaming yourself for anything unpleasant and thinking that everything people say or do is a reaction to you. You take too much responsibility for other people's feelings and behavior.

(e.g. "My wife came home in a bad mood: it must be something I did." Or "I know you all hate me now because I was such an ass last week in group.") How have I "taken it personally" when it probably wasn't about me?

May 1

My favorite way to spend the day is...

May 2

If I could talk to my young child, the one
thing I would say is...

May 3

The two moments I'll never forget in my life are... describe them in great detail, and what makes them so unforgettable.

May 4

The words I'd like to live by are...

May 5

When I'm in pain ☐ physical or emotional ☐
the kindest thing I can do for myself is...

May 6

Make a list of the people in your life who
genuinely support you, and who you can
genuinely trust.

May 7

What does unconditional love look like for you?

May 8

What would you do if you loved yourself unconditionally? How can you act on these things whether you do or don't?

May 9

I really wish others knew this about me...

May 10

If my body could talk, it would say...

May 11

Using 10 words, describe yourself. Go back through each word and write a reasoning for each choice.

May 12

What can you learn from your biggest mistakes?

May 13

I feel most energized when...

May 14

Make a list of everything you'd like to say "no" to.

May 15
Make a list of everything you'd like to say "yes" to.

May 16
Write the words you want to hear about yourself.

74

May 17

List three things you'd do if you weren't so afraid.

May 18

Nobody knows this about me...

May 19

Is there a particular worry that you can't shake? How do you cope with worry?

May 20

Write a "Dear Mom" letter (for self or sharing with others in recovery).

May 21

Write a "Dear Dad" letter (for self or sharing with others in recovery).

May 22

Write a letter to yourself as a "child" and how
you would have nurtured him/her.

May 23

Write a letter to yourself for the future.

May 24

Describe the traits you like about yourself.

May 25

Describe a situation that makes you come "alive".

May 26

When it comes to body image, what are things you wish could change about yourself?

May 27

How did you feel shame about your body or sexuality growing up?

May 28

How did your family play together (i.e. hiking, board games, etc.)? If nothing comes to mind, what would you have wanted?

May 29

What dreams did you have of yourself growing up?

May 30

What dreams do you have of yourself now?

May 31

How would you describe your relationship to peers in school, sports, etc.? (i.e. did you fit in, feel awkward, teased/bullied, etc.)

June 1

What was the most hurtful thing a friend, classmate, or peer either said about you or did to you growing up?

June 2

In what ways has your addiction made you more vulnerable, and in what ways has it make you less vulnerable?

June 3

What are things you can do in 15 minutes or less that improve your mood?

June 4

When was a time you felt content? What made you feel that way and how can you regain that feeling?

June 5

How do you handle rejection/fear/grief/other negative emotions? How can you be more prepared for those times in the future?

June 6

What has recovery from addiction taught you about your past?

June 7
3 things I value about myself are?

June 8
Something I would like to do but not sure if I could pull it off is...

June 9

If I eat when I'm not hungry, I'm most likely
to be feeling....

June 10

Who are/were your favorite relatives and why?

June 11

What activities bring you joy/a sense of completeness?

June 12

What's something you wish you knew about your parents?

June 13

What one talent or skill you wish you had?

June 14

What one talent or skill others admire about you?

June 15
Draw out your emotions (i.e. what you're feeling) using paint or colored markers.

June 16

Think of a time you did something you didn't think you could do? What were the circumstances and feelings going into it? How do you feel or learn after accomplishing this feat?

June 17

What image or metaphor best represents your current path in life? (e.g. "A phoenix rising from the ashes") Please elaborate on your choice.

June 18

Draw a place (real or imagined) that makes you feel safe.

June 19

Draw yourself as an animal. What animal do you feel you have a kindred relationship with.

June 20

List 5 positive moments in childhood (i.e. birth–18 yrs. old)

June 21

List 5 negative moments in childhood.

June 22

List 5 positive moments in adulthood.

June 23

List 5 negative moments in adulthood.

June 24

Create a timeline of your life and list all the significant events that occurred. (2 pages please)

101

June 25

Look at a young picture of yourself. What do
you see? How would you describe the emotions
occurring within the picture? What emotions
are stirred now as you look at yourself?

June 26

What's your favorite quote and why?

June 27

Write a Haiku about yourself or recovery? (i.e. three lines with 5, 7, 5 syllables in each line)

June 28

What are lyrics from a song that moves you?

June 29

Write a list of all things you do to escape?

June 30

Have you ever had a spiritual experience?
Please describe it.

July 1

Keep a list of your day's sexual thoughts, feelings, fantasies, pre-occupations, etc. (i.e. analogous to a food log where you track these in relation to time, moods, environment)

July 2

List out your inner circle ("bottom-line behaviors") and middle circle behaviors (i.e. behaviors that can be "on-ramps" to inner circle such as FB, Craigslist, channel surfing, certain movies/magzines, websites, etc.)

July 3

List 10 moments or experiences where you
felt "powerless" or when your life became
"unmanageable" over your addiction/compulsive
sexual behaviors.

July 4

List at least 10 specific "problems" associated
with your addiction/sexual behaviors.

July 5

List at least 5 negative cognitions or "core beliefs" you have about yourself ("I'm unlovable, don't deserve a healthy relationship, etc). For each one you should list an example of it in childhood (i.e. growing up in your family of origin) and one in adulthood.

July 6

Write out how shame (i.e. cultural, family, societal, etc.) played in your addiction and in your efforts to seek help. Remember shame is about feeling bad, defective, and worthless and believing you should be punished vs. healthy guilt which is focused on the rectifying behaviors.

July 7

List specifically what your sexually compulsive behaviors are and what you received from each type of the experience (i.e. validation, affirmation, ego boost, etc.)

July 8

87% of sex addicts report other addictions so how do other addictions play into your sexual addiction? If you're unaware, what addiction or compulsive behavior would most likely be used as a substitute if you were to go without a sexual one?

July 9

Sex addicts tend to come from families with addiction so please share what other addictions or compulsive/detaching behaviors occur within your family (please start with your grandparents, aunts and uncles, and work towards your current nuclear family with your parents and siblings).

July 10

Describe how affection and emotional expression was or was not shared in your family and the impact it had on your ability to share your emotions. (i.e. hugs, "I love you", emotional space for sadness, anger, fear, etc.)

July 11

Write a relapse scenario that could realistically cause you to relapse back into your addiction. Please make this detailed to include triggers, events, situations, relationships, that can impact a relapse.

July 12

Since addiction goes hand-in-hand with co-dependency, list ways you struggled with being honest with your partner/spouse for fear of losing her (i.e. setting boundaries, wanting to say "no" but agreeing anyways, etc).

July 13

When did you hit "rock bottom"? Why do you consider this event/moment your bottom?

July 14

How does entitlement play into your addiction? (i.e. feeling like you "deserve" it)

July 15

Who else outside your recovery circle (i.e. therapist, spouse, family, group members) knows about your addiction? How did you share this to them and what was the experience like? If no one, what do you think you are afraid of?

July 16
Describe your top 3 proudest moments?

July 17
List both the positive and negative qualities of your father.

July 18
List both the positive and negative qualities
of your mother.

July 19
Describe how you feel about your mother.

July 20

What emotions does she express openly and how?

July 21

Describe how you and your mother communicate.

July 22

List the most pleasant and unpleasant
experiences with your mother (up to 5 each).

July 23
What was your mother's goal for your life?

July 24
Describe how you feel about your father.

July 25

What emotions does he express openly and how?

July 26

Describe how you and your father communicate?

July 27

List the most pleasant and unpleasant experiences with your father (up to 5 each).

July 28

What was your father's goal for your life?

July 29

List 5 of your most disturbing events or experiences in your childhood.

July 30
What unresolved issues or feelings do you have
with your mother?

July 31
What unresolved issues or feelings do you have
with your father?

August 1

I deserve love because...

August 2

I am a good person because...

August 3

I am lovable because...

August 4

I can be trusted because...

August 5

I can trust myself because...

August 6

I am now in control because...

August 7
I can safely feel (show) my emotions
because...

August 8
I can make my needs known because...

August 9

I am significant because...

August 10

Write a letter to a loved one.

August 11

Reflect on your career. Jot down a timeline of it, including all the ups and downs. What was your best experience? And the worst? What would you like your future to look like, in terms of your career? If you haven't started a career yet, focus on that future part. What do you want your work to look like?

August 12

Read this quote and write how you feel about
it: "Far better is it to dare mighty things, to
win glorious triumphs, even though checkered
by failure... than to rank with those poor
spirits who neither enjoy nor suffer much,
because they live in a gray twilight that
knows not victory nor defeat." -Theodore
Roosevelt

August 13

Write out your day (events, feelings, experiences, etc.) If you write in the morning then reflect on the past day.

August 14

What feelings come up when you think about death/mortality? What about what legacy you'd like to leave behind?

August 15

Write whatever comes to mind for 5-10 minutes. We call this "stream-of-consciousness" writing.

August 16

Who is a role-model for you and why?

August 17

Read the quote and write about how it impact your life: "Until you heal the wounds of your past, you will continue to bleed. You can bandage the bleeding with food, with alcohol, with drugs, with work, with cigarettes, with sex, but eventually, it will all ooze through and stain your life. You must find the strength to open the wounds, stick your hands inside, pull out the core of the pain that is holding you in your past, the memories, and make peace with them." ☐Iyanla Vanzant

August 18

How do you identify with this quote:
"Eventually you will come to understand that
love heals everything, and love is all there is."
— Gary Zukav

August 19

"Healing is a matter of time, but it is sometimes also a matter of opportunity." — Hippocrates

What does "opportunity" mean to you in recovery?

August 20

"Healing may not be so much about getting better, as about letting go of everything that isn't you — all of the expectations, all of the beliefs — and becoming who you are." — Rachel Naomi Remen

Many addicts in recovery have gone through a lifetime of living up to other's expectations or beliefs about who they are or should be. How does this apply to you?

August 21

"Our sorrows and wounds are healed only when we touch them with compassion." — Buddha

Are you able to look at your past wounds and be compassionate with yourself? Or do you dismiss the past or just "deal with it" without grieving the pain? Please explain.

August 22

"Healing doesn't mean the damage never existed. It means the damage no longer controls our lives." — Anonymous

Some people may erroneously believe healing may mean either ignoring past pain or denying of its existence. How have you seen your "damage" controlling less of you?

August 23

"I now see how owning our story and loving ourselves through that process is the bravest thing that we will ever do." — Anonymous

What would it look like for you to "own" your story? If you feel you've accomplished this, what would you share to others who haven't done so? What was the process like for you to go from shaming yourself to loving yourself?

August 24

"Your struggle is part of your story." —
Anonymous

Have you learned to embrace your struggle? If
not what's making it difficult? If so, what
does this mean for you?

August 25

"Unexpressed emotions will never die. They are buried alive and will come forth later in uglier ways." Anonymous

What unexpressed emotions still reside within you?

August 26

"The curious paradox is that when I accept myself just as I am, then I can change." — Carl Rogers

Change usually happens when you learn to unconditionally accept yourself. This means accepting your past, and well as your present. How has your recovery reflected this? If not, what's holding you back from true acceptance of self?

August 27

"Don't let your struggle become your identity." - Anonymous

While I use the term "addict" in my writing, I truly hope you don't see that as your main identity. I want people to recognize that in recovery, the "addict" label is just a part what comprises them. At no point should an addict feel this is one's "calling card" to the world. How do you relate to this?

August 28

"Not until we are lost do we begin to understand ourselves." — Henry David Thoreau

Many addicts can remember a time of being so lost in their addictions it felt utterly incomprehensible as to why they do what they do. But only after walking in darkness do they stumble upon the light. How do you identify with this quote?

August 29

"We know what we are, but know not what we may be." — William Shakespeare

Some recovering addicts see sobriety as the final destination. But this stops short of finding a higher calling to your life. What do you think your life can be beyond just sobriety?

August 30

"We must let go of the life we have planned,
so as to accept the one that is waiting for
us." — Joseph Campbell

Have you accepted the life that is currently
upon you or are you still trying to hang on to
the one you had envisioned or planned?

August 31

"You are never too old to set another goal or dream another dream." — C.S. Lewis

Can you think of a dream/goal you want to see accomplished?

September 1
Listen to a soothing song of your choice.
Write about this experience.

September 2
Take a 20 minute bath. Describe in writing
how it felt.

September 3

Take 5 minutes to do some deep breathing
while paying attention to your body starting
from your toes and ending with your head.
Now write down what you noticed regarding
your bodily sensations (i.e. muscle tension,
aches, etc.)

September 4

Is there a new way you can forgive yourself?
Is there anything you haven't totally forgiven
yourself for in the past and why?

September 5

The two moments I'll never forget in my life are... Describe them in great detail, and what makes them so unforgettable.

September 6

When I'm in pain □ physical or emotional □ the kindest thing I can do for myself is...

September 7

I really wish others knew this about me...

September 8

What are your views on religion/spirituality?
How does that impact your recovery?

September 9

Who knows the most about you? Who do you
want to know more about you? What makes it
difficult to make that happen.

September 10

What friend do you miss and why?

September 11
What's something you disagree with regarding
the way you were raised?

September 12
What country would you like to visit for peace
and relaxation?

September 13

What are two things or situations that make you nervous or uncomfortable?

September 14

Have you ever felt like you were meant for something, that some event or moment in your life was fated? Have you ever felt an inexplicable call to do something? Where do you think this feeling comes from? Write about it.

September 15
What are you grateful for?

September 16
How well do you take feedback/criticism?

September 17
Addiction goes hand-in-hand with codependency. How codependent have you been? What's changed?

September 18
How difficult is it to accept a compliment? Some addicts often dismiss or minimize a compliment. Please share your experience.

September 19

Similar to difficulty in accepting compliments, addicts may struggle with apologizing profusely for various minor things. How true is this in your life?

September 20

What wrong assumptions do people often make about you?

September 21

Are you comfortable "doing nothing
productive"? How has this changed over time?

September 22

What are your views on the phrase, "Everything
happens for a reason"?

September 23
How has Social Media impacted your addiction
recovery (i.e. for better and for worse)?

September 24
How do you handle triggering scenes in movies
or advertising?

September 25

What are your sleep habits (i.e. regular, erratic, etc.)? Do you get enough sleep or do you often find yourself tired or exhausted? What can you do to change this?

September 26

How does eating impact your recovery? Do you ever eat when you're extremely triggered or have "emotional eating" moments?

September 27
Think of your dreams and write about any recurring themes, patterns, or worries.

September 28
What does courage mean to you and what does it look like in your recovery?

September 29

What is your greatest fear and why? Is this rooted in the past?

September 30

What do you dislike most about your appearance? How have you learned to accept this part of you with compassion?

September 31
What is an experience in your life that you consider to be a miracle?

October 1
What's your best memory of school during childhood?

October 2

What's your worst memory of school during childhood?

October 3

What's the highlight of your past week?

October 4

What's one thing you want to do or accomplish before your next birthday?

October 5

Who's the one person who supports you the most in your life (intellectually and emotionally)?

October 6

What do you find yourself feeling obligated to
do? How long have you felt this way and why
does it happen?

October 7

What book has most impacted your life and
why?

171

October 8

What's something you collect or hoard? Is this a healthy outlet for you or does it have to be re-examined?

October 9

What's something you're pessimistic about?

October 10
What do you like best about yourself?

October 11
What makes you feel safe?

October 12
When are you happiest?

October 13
Describe something that makes you feel peaceful?

October 14

What is something you are optimistic about?

October 15

What is something you are pessimistic about?

October 16

Write from a spouse or significant other's perspective on how your addiction has impacted them.

October 17

When I get angry it's usually because...

October 18

When I get down on myself it's usually
because...

October 19

What pressures do you face regularly?

October 20

Beyond addiction, how have you been prone to escapism?

October 21

What fictional (movie, t.v., book, cartoon, etc.) father would you like to have and why?

October 22

What does "rock-bottom" mean to you and have you experienced it?

October 23

When was the last time someone whole-
heartedly asked for your forgiveness? If you
can't recall, think of a time you asked for
someone's forgiveness? How did you feel
afterwards?

October 24

Shame is about self-condemnation whereas guilt is looking at the actions and behaviors separate from self? Are you able to view your actions less from a shame perspective? What has helped? If not, what's hindering the process?

October 25

Think of a time you were extremely critical of yourself. What did you do and why did it bother you/others?

October 26

Think of a time you were extremely critical of someone else? What did they do and why did it bother you?

October 27

If you still suffer from toxic shame what steps can you be taking towards healing?

October 28

To have power over others, I often...

October 29

To get attention, I often...

October 30

To gain prestige or status, I often...

October 31

Describe a time you felt excluded and unaccepted. What feelings come up as you revisit this?

November 1

How was forgiveness expressed in your family growing up? How does this affect you today?

November 2

Read the story of the "Cracked Pot" and share your feelings:

There is a story about a water bearer in India who had two large pots. Each hung on the ends of a pole that he carried across his neck. One of the pots had a small crack in it but the other pot was perfect and always delivered a full portion of water at the end of the long walk from the stream to the master's house, but the pot that was broken near its bottom arrived only half full.

For two years this went on daily, with the bearer delivering only one and a half pots full of water to his master's house. Of course, the perfect pot was proud of its accomplishments, and bragged constantly about its full measure of water when it arrived. But the poor broken pot was ashamed of its imperfection, and miserable that it was able to retain only half of what it was supposed to hold.

After two years of what it perceived to be a bitter failure, it spoke to the water bearer one day by the stream.

"I am ashamed of myself, and I want to apologize to you."

"Why?" asked the bearer. "What are you ashamed of?", asked the water bearer. "I have been able, for these past two years, to carry only half my load because this crack that I am afflicted with causes water to leak out all the way back to your master. Because of my flaws, you have to do all of this work, and you don't get full value from your efforts," the pot said.

The water bearer felt sorry for the poor broken pot, and in his compassion he said, "As we return to the master's house, I want you to notice the beautiful flowers along the path." As they went up the hill, the old pot noticed the sun warming some beautiful wild flowers on the side of the path, and this cheered the pot a little. But at the end of the trail, it still felt bad because it had leaked out half its load, and so again it apologized to the bearer for its failure.

186

The bearer said to the pot, "Did you notice that there were flowers only on your side of your path, but not on the other pot's side? That's because I have always known about your flaw, and I took advantage of it. I planted flower seeds on your side of the path, and every day while we walk back from the stream, you've watered them. For two years I have been able to pick these beautiful flowers to decorate my master's table. Without you being just the way you are, my master would not have this beauty to grace his house." -Anonymous

November 3

Describe what you want your life to look like in 5 years.

November 4

Find a photo album of your childhood. Choose 2-3 pictures that resonate with you. How do you feel when looking at yourself in these pictures? What memories come to mind? Anything your adult side would tell the child side of you?

November 5

What are the top 3 websites you visit and why? Is this conducive to your recovery?

November 6

Describe a time you felt really alone?

November 7

How do you keep yourself accountable from relapse?

November 8

Write about your addiction from a 3rd person perspective (e.g. "Jim's addiction started when he was 10 years old...).

November 9

The most recent time I felt sad was...

November 10

The physical sensations that I felt when I felt sad included...

November 11

If or when I raise children I will never...

November 12

What is your favorite hobby? Why do you enjoy
it and how often are you able to participate
in it?

November 13

Write about a time your parents embarrassed you?

November 14

What makes you proud to be in recovery?

November 15

What is your definition of success?

November 16

What is your definition of true recovery?

November 17

When did you last feel helpless and what did you do about it?

November 18

When was the last time someone said they were proud of you? Describe the situation.

November 19

What role does competition play in your life? Are you competitive that you feel you must win vs. want to win? How do you handle losing?

November 20

In what ways have you not been able to control your addictive behaviors despite repeated attempts to do so?

November 21

Please give examples of "euphoric recall" (i.e. thoughts or feelings of exhilaration or a high) based on your addiction.

November 22

Were your parents or grandparents physically affectionate? Other extended members in your family?

November 23

Were you touched in a nurturing, loving way by your mother/father? If not, your feelings on this loss? How did it impact your parenting (if you're not a parent please think of how you would respond if you did have children)?

November 24

How emotionally available were your parents during your childhood?

November 25

Were you ever called names growing up? If so what were the names and how did they make you feel?

November 26

Did your parents/caregivers ever tell negative or "put down" stories about you?

November 27

What was your family role? (i.e. mascot, hero/responsible child, black sheep, lost/invisible child, etc.) Describe the impact on you as a child and as an adult?

November 28

Were you given adult chores or responsibilities beyond your age level? (e.g. making dinner for yourself and siblings)

November 29

Were you ever locked in a room or closet intentionally or excessively? Please jot down the feelings and impact.

November 30

Describe an item you were attached to as a child. What happened to it?

December 1
Share an imperfection about yourself that you now cherish.

December 2
How difficult is it to ask someone to do a favor for you? When was the last time you asked? Why do you think this is an issue? Where does it stem from?

203

December 3

Share a time when you were really jealous of someone. Did you act on it?

December 4

Do you like your name? What's the story behind it?

December 5

When you're sick or hurt, do you allow others
to care for you or do you soldier it alone as
a way not to "bother" people? What would it
take for you to ask for help?

December 6

Describe a time where you felt a "spiritual"
moment or experience?

December 7

"The tragedy of life is what dies inside a man
while he lives." —Albert Schweitzer
How does this quote apply to your life?

December 8

What's the biggest risk you've taken in life?
What did you learn from this experience?

December 9

Write a letter to your addict by starting it off with, "Dear Addict". (share about the lies the addict has told you in addition to the pain of saying good-bye to the addict)

December 10

When I look in the mirror I see....

December 11

There's this phrase in recovery, "Once an addict, always an addict". How do you feel about this? What does it mean to you?

208

December 12

Set a timer and close your eyes. Now spend the next 5 minutes breathing and trying to empty your mind (i.e. thoughts and feelings) by focusing on your bodily sensations. What came up for you? How was this experience?

December 13

What's your biggest regret and why?

December 14

Describe the last time you were surprised by an intense feeling you had that you didn't expect to happen.

December 15

Share a time in childhood where you felt unsafe?

December 16

What conversation did you overhear in childhood that you wish you didn't?

December 17

Write about a time in childhood where you were left alone to fend for yourself in an overwhelming situation. How did that feel? What was the outcome?

December 18

What is one affirmation you'd like to give yourself? Has anyone shared a similar affirmation with you?

December 19

What am I excited about right now in my life?

December 20

Trace your work history. When did you first
make money? How did you feel about it then?
How do view money now? What were you
taught about money and work (i.e. relationship
between work, money, and masculinity)? Is
your work a place for you to just collect a
paycheck or are you genuinely thriving?

December 21

What can you do today that you were not capable of one year ago? How does this make you feel?

December 22

If you could take a single photo to represent your life what would it look like and why?

December 23

What skills, talents, or abilities are you thankful you have?

December 24

How do you measure your value? What determines your worth?

December 25

What positive things about you do you find hard to accept?

December 26

What commitments or activities are you engaged in where you need to take a break due to feeling emotionally drained or just no longer interested in helping?

December 27

What do you need more clarity about? How can you get it?

December 28

What do you want to trust yourself more about?

December 29

What real and honest conversation do you
need to have either with a partner or trusted
friend?

December 30

What makes you feel relaxed? When was the
last time you experienced this? Is this
something you need to implement more of in
your life and if so how can you make it
happen?

December 31

Reflect on your journal writing from this past year. Anything stick out? What do you want to change for the next year?

Proof